Presented to the
Gilmer County Public Library

Knowledge Moves Mountains   Knowledge Moves Mountains

Donated by

The Author

Half Them Lies Is True
Simple Cowboy Poetry

Quentin M. Thomas

AKA *Texas Red*

Acknowledgements

No project like this is complete without giving thanks to those who encouraged, supported, and persevered through the process.

My wife Suzie has listened to more cowboy poems and ideas than any mortal should have to endure. She is my love, a constant source of encouragement to all of my projects and my best friend. My girls, Julie and Tracy, are also to be thanked.

A special thanks goes to my cousin, Richard Sparks, who did the illustrations. He is a lifelong trouble making friend. He is also the most gifted artists that I know. We are forever Texans and cowboys at heart. His encouragement was invaluable.

Table of Contents

Introduction   1
Poetry My Way   7
Half Them Lies Is True   9
A Cowboy To The End   13
A Place Called Texas   17
G.T.T.   19
I'm A Native Texan   23
Texas If You Please   25
Please Bury Me In Texas   27
Within The Arms Of God   29
The Ringling Stage   33
Devil Horse   35
Don't Judge A Horse By Its Looks   37
Be Careful Where You Race   41
That Indian Kid   45
Charlie Parkhurst,
    Stage Coach Driver   47
Just A Boy Of Ten   49
Common Sense   53
Stage Coach West   55
Crossing Of The Red   59
The Fall Of 81   63
Ole Red On Ice   67
The Mighty Chisholm Trail   69
That's What A Cowboy'd Say   71
The Dime Novel   75
Shorty And The Fight   77
The Llano Estacado   81
Look Out Dodge City   83
Rolling Smokes   85
The Last Game   87

The Coming Of The Wire   91
The Slicker With The Mouth   93
The Wiry Kid   97
It's Winter At The Ranch   101
Changing Of The West   103
Who Really Won The West   107
Saddle'n-up Time   109
Memorial Hill   113
Would You Believe?   115
The Lacey Hat   117
Nature's Church   121
He Was Just A Cowboy   123
Ashes In The Wind   125
Waiting At The Gate   127
You Know I'll Make A Hand   129
Educated Cowboys   131

INTRODUCTION

Throughout American history few eras have had the lasting romantic and appeal as the period between 1865 and 1895. This was the general era of the open range and the heyday of the American cowboy. Many young men dreamed of adventure in the old west and the excitement was directly reflected in the cowboy lifestyle, dress, and personality. They were young, some even pre-teen as they rode up the trail. Most were uneducated by contemporary standards but wise to the ways of the range. The cowboy was a wonderful mix of Spanish Conquistador, Mexican Vaquero, Texas independence and a healthy helping of bullheaded, hardworking Native American.

While the cowboy has had a lasting impact on Americans the positive impact on other parts of the globe is not to be discounted. In Europe, Western novels are very popular. German author, Karl May wrote about the open range era on the Llano Estacado of West Texas. This generated tremendous interest in the American West. Interestingly, his descriptions and characters were so graphic that today Germans still come to Texas and the Great Staked plains (Llano Estacado) to view the geographical wonders and the historic locations that May described in his novels. This interest and intrigue is based on novels written by an author that never visited the region in person.

Today you can find cowboys, head & heeling, cutting and paint branding on many weekends in Hawaii. One of the largest ranches under individual name, the Parker Ranch, is located on the big island of Hawaii. With the exception of the colorful hatbands and palaka plaid shirts they could be in any arena in west Texas. The cowboy spirit persists world-wide even today.

It goes without saying that John Wayne and Clint Eastwood have carried the image (true or false) worldwide in hundreds of western movies. Today the legend continues. Actors like Robert Duvall, Kevin Costner, Tom Selleck, Tommy Lee Jones and Sam Elliott are western icons. Movies such as "Lonesome Dove," "Monty Walsh," "Open Range" and "You Know My Name" have gone a long way towards providing an accurate portrayal of the real cowboy era.

While the Spanish Vaquero may well be the original American cowboy, it all started in earnest following the Civil War, as soldiers returned to their homes, they found little waiting for them except hard work. However, during the war the rangy Longhorn cows ran wild thorough the central and western regions of Texas and had multiplied tremendously. Since there were virtually no organized ranches, the cattle were free for the taking. If you had a good cow pony, a saddle, a rope, a branding iron and willingness for hard work you could start a spread on some of the millions of acres of open range.

With the increasing American appetite for beef in the eastern states, the cattle had to be moved to the markets such as Chicago. It was soon determined that driving cattle that far was impossible. Driving them to closer locations that allowed the use of other available transportation such as ships was equally as difficult and could not economically meet the increasing demand.

At about this same time the American railroads were moving across the southern portion of Kansas. Entrepreneurial men like Joseph G. McCoy encouraged the railroads to build farther and farther west. Simultaneously, he was coaxing the Texas cattlemen to drive their beef to the anticipated railhead towns. It didn't take long for enterprising cowboys to realize that these shorter drives were the perfect solution. Out of the heart of Texas originated trails that would become famous in history. The Shawnee, the Western, the Goodnight-Loving and the Chisholm trails became famous. Towns and cattlemen became famous for their support of this effort. Fort Worth, Texas is still known as Cowtown USA. During the years of the great trail drives millions of Longhorns grazed their way to the Kansas railhead markets.

Eventually, the railheads reached points in the south like Fort Worth, Texas. Available transportation, local meatpacking houses and refrigerated railcars coupled with the increased use of barbed wire doomed the great trail drives. As a result of this historic twenty to thirty year era, all the great ranges of America from south Texas to Montana were populated by Texas livestock.

While the great drives are no more, the cowboy still survives. In Texas alone there are a number of great ranches with wonderful rich histories. They include: the Four Sixes, the Pitchfork and the King Ranch and others. These are not just ranches; they are Texas institutions where cowboys still practice their trade on a daily basis. Some things have changed and there are instances where technology is lending a hand to the tried and true ways of the early West. However, it is not uncommon to see a cowboy on a good cow pony, leg cocked across his saddle horn, hat tilted just so, sitting solitary on the range "checking the stock or weather." If you are a cowboy at heart it will cause you to momentarily reflect back 150 years. Go for it; let the spirit take you away.

The musings in this book are a collection of thoughts gathered over a number of years. They are provided as my offering because I am a native Texan who owns a small piece of Texas that is on the Chisholm Trail. I have a longtime love for Texas and the American West. I write with a sincere appreciation and respect for the contributions of all of the cowboys of yesterday and today. To this special group of men who were mostly young, often rough around the edges, hardworking, colorful and worn-out long before their time, it goes without saying that this country owes a great debt of gratitude to the cowboy who has become not only an American icon but our ambassador to the entire world.

It is my hope you will enjoy these humble efforts from a Texas cowboy at heart.

Quentin M. Thomas
AKA *Texas Red*

It is a unique stage of life when an individual is comfortable with their accomplishments and can confidently apply those lessons learned without fear of failure or criticism.

Texas Red

Poetry My Way

The cowboy life is simple,
So the poetry ain't too hard.
And fancy words that just don't rhyme,
Don't come from this here bard.

If words ain't got no tempo,
They're so much prose to me.
They gotta have a little rhyme,
To be good poetry.

If they don't tell a waddie's tale,
Bout cows and guns and guts.
Ain't much use to me you see,
Won't like them very much.

A cowboys got no learning,
So it's up there in their head.
Lord knows if they'd just study some,
They'd read their rhymes instead.

Most times they're true, sometimes
they're not,
I don't know I care.
But rhyme they must each second line,
Or poetry just ain't there.

If you're gonna do it....do it right.

Texas Red

The Comanches' horsemanship impressed the cowmen. "The young warriors on bareback ponies would ride all over the horses backs...off on one side, standing up, lying down...going at full speed."

L.D. Taylor
Rancher

Half Them Lies Is True

He was standing at bar center,
His heel hung on the rail.
Knocking back that rot gut,
And spinning Wild West tales.

His hat was tilted on his head,
His gun a forty-four.
His elbows resting on the bar,
You could hear him rail and roar.

He told about them Texas spreads,
He'd wrangled for them all.
From Brownsville up to Lodgepole,
He'd heard them doggies bawl.

He used to hunt the buffalo,
Was at Adobe Walls.
Seen that shot a thousand yards,
Seen that Indian fall.

He once met the brothers Earp,
Played cards till nearly two.
Knew Bat and Doc and all the boys,
While he was in his youth.

He rode once with the Rangers,
Down near the Rio Grande.
Ran cows out of the Brazos breaks,
And feared no living man.

Stood ground with C.C. Slaughter
On the Llano way out west.
Been to hell's half acre,
His life had stood the test.

Rode the Chisholm across the Red,
The Goodnight-Loving too.
Seen blizzards up near Judith Gap,
But pushed them doggies through.

This cowboy railed on through the night,
A story, then one more.
He knocked back one more glass of rye,
And headed for the door.

He stumbled walking down the steps,
But swung onto his bay.
Gave a spur and spun around,
And he was on his way.

The boys laughed hard about them tales,
A know-it-all they guessed.
A waddie past his prime in life
His stories were the best.

The foreman turned to all the room,
The place went kind of quiet.
He'd listened to the stories all,
For almost half the night.

"I've known the man for 20 years,
Those tales we've often shared.
Most was true with some a stretch,
I don't know I care."

"Men like him don't come along,
But once among a few.
He lived a life of open range,
When this here West was new."

"He set a mark that most men miss,
Across this western land.
His word's his bond, he's paid his dues,
My friend and one top hand."

The cow boss took his final glass,
His stare could look you through.
"Waddies, you best listen up
Cause half them lies is true!"

There is nothing stronger than a few good men dedicated to a worthy cause... and with grit to get it done.

Texas Red

A Cowboy To The End

Ole Bill had always been around,
A fixture you might say.
He swept the floor, did odd jobs,
Was never in the way.

The barkeep kept him busy,
With work around the place.
He shined spittoons, wiped tables down,
Just never had a face.

He wore a beat up Stetson,
His pants could use a mend.
His shirt was frayed and tattered,
And his boots was wearing thin.

His look was one of times gone past,
His hat was creased old style.
His boots high top the Texas way,
He'd give the boys a smile.

The young bucks they would ride him
hard,
When they were at the bar.
Forgetting he was them some day,
They often went too far.

His work he did as best he could,
To make a buck or two.
A little room was his out back,
When all his work was through.

He didn't have a family,
Least none the locals knew.
No tack, no gun, no earthly stuff,
His worldly goods were few.

Some said he'd rode the biggest brands,
When he was fresh and young.
Rode up the trail for fifteen years,
Was handy with a gun.

One night the bar was packed and loud,
The crews all gathered round.
To have some drinks and have some fun,
To spend some time in town.

Then outside we heard some shots,
From down by Stephen's store.
We headed for the window,
To see what caused the roar.

Among the loud commotion,
A buckboard rig broke loose.
With lady and her youngster,
And wild and spooked Cayuse.

And down the street that rig lit out,
Hell bent for who knows where.
With the lady and her youngster,
Behind that crazy mare.

While everyone was gawking,
A wondering what to do.
A single man took action,
And from the crowd broke through.

Ole Bill jumped for that frightened mare,
The bravest thing I've seen.
He grabbed for tack and grabbed for
mane,
He grabbed for anything.

What happened next gets cloudy,
But the rig came to a stop.
Bill had slipped beneath a wheel,
But the reins he didn't drop.

We pulled him out but he was gone,
The doctor did his best.
But Bill was tired and slipped away,
Into his final rest.

So till the last a cowboy,
He died a hero's death.
He saved that lady and her child,
He gave till his last breath.

I guess that he's a riding now,
On God's great open range.
A looking good and sitting tall,
No worries to complain.

And I guess in reflection,
When I gotta check it in.
I'd like to go like Bill did,
A cowboy to the end.

I'd rather have a man's true friendship than any other gift.

Texas Red

Hire the man with the well-stained sweat band.

Texas Red

"Gentlemen wear spurs in a saloon, but never in a friend's house."

Old cowboy saying

A Place Called Texas
(The Master's Perfect Plan)

When God laid out the universe,
There was lots he had to do.
He started slow to get the knack,
And got better as it grew.

He made the moon and made the sun,
Some light to see his work.
He made the stars and planets,
And then he made the earth.

The good book says he made it all,
The sea, the sky, the land.
He made the creatures big and small,
And then he made a man.

He looked around this floating sphere,
Something it just weren't right.
He felt he could do better,
So he thought with all his might.

Then like a flash it came to him,
He knew just what to do.
He'd make a place just perfect,
Before his work was through.

This place it must be perfect,
Through-out eternity.
It would be his masterpiece,
For everyone to see.

It had to have some mountains,
And rivers to the sea.
Rolling plains and rich sunsets,
He clapped his hands with glee.

He knew what he was doing,
And he knew he had it right.
Perfection don't come with ease,
He'd work with all his might.

So he rolled his sleeves, he took a breath,
And then he dove right in.
So many works to choose from,
Just where should he begin.

He made the rolling Brazos,
The mighty Rio Grande.
The Red, the Bend, the Llano,
With sweeping vistas grand.

But God he wasn't finished,
He made the pine woods.
The plains out near El Paso,
Where timeless mountains stood.

He made the rolling hills up north,
The Trinity fed the land.
The oceans and the islands,
The wonders of his hand.

It isn't hard to look around,
And see his mighty hand.
He made a place called Texas,
The Master's perfect plan.

G.T.T.

G.T.T. was on the door,
They're leaving here for good.
Gone to Texas one and all,
Was clearly understood.

Our wagons loaded to the brim,
With chickens, kids and wife.
We're headed West to Texas,
We leave at dawns first light.

Cause times is hard and crops is poor,
We done the best we could.
We worked this place from dawn to
dusk,
The land's just no darn good.

We owe for land, we owe for seed,
The bills just can't be paid.
We're pulling stakes and headed west,
Our mind has done been made.

They say there's land for all that's free,
Just stake and make your mark.
The Mexicans has leagues and leagues,
We'll make a brand new start.

The water runs both pure and clear,
There's game to shoot and eat.
With rolling hills and endless plains,
Rich sod beneath our feet.

It's like the earth is fresh and young,
Said the trapper at the store.
Most likely he was stretching some,
But it could be much more.

Could be Injuns here and there,
No need to worry none.
Them Rangers keep'em chased away,
And we brought this here gun.

We'll cut some logs and build a place,
The first year might be tough.
We'll plant our crops and kill some
game,
We're Southern and we're tough.

They say that God has blessed this
place,
And folks can prosper there.
The land spreads out for miles and
miles,
And them Mexicans they is fair.

We'll have to say we go to Mass,
We'll give a wink and nod.
My guess is they don't really care,
We pray to just one God.

So off we go with kids and all,
We'll leave this place behind.
We're gone to Texas, headed West,
And life will be so fine.

So as we leave, like I just said,
We'll mark it on the door.
Gone to Texas one and all,
We won't be back no more.

You make your luck by being prepared for opportunities.

𝒯𝑒𝓍𝒶𝓈 𝑅𝑒𝒹

I'm A Native Texan

I'm a native Texan,
I guess that you can tell.
Cause I don't try to hide it,
And I wear it oh so well.

Some things reflect my birthright,
And most folks plainly see.
There's something in my manner,
It's proud and spirit free.

But many lead the way to here,
Before I came along.
I'll share some of my heritage,
With words ... just come along.

Adventures come from frontier blood,
Austin blazed the trail.
Hard leadership came from Houston,
Some men the world knows well.

A legacy of Spanish roots,
Blood lines rich and old.
Our courage from the Alamo,
All men with spirits bold.

Rangers gave us bravery,
While farmers tilled the land.
Keen cattle skills Vaqueros gave,
To Anglo waddie bands.

The spirit came from cowboys young,
The range and Chisholm Trail.
Their legacy continues,
All nations sing their tales.

State, nation and republic,
Our single star held high.
We pray to rest in Texas,
When it comes our time to die.

I have said some times before,
When God comes back you see.
Please bury me in Texas,
Cause that's where he'll look for me.

Texas If You Please

Now I could go to Big Bend,
There ain't no people there.
Except down near Terlingua,
When chili's in the air.

The piney woods of Texas east,
That place is oh so fair.
The coastal plains near Corpus,
The beach and salty air.

Now, way up on the Llano,
With miles where you can roam.
No trees to hide a headstone,
The buffalo called it home.

The Alamo still draws me back,
Where Texas legends dwell.
The limestone creeks and natural
springs,
Among the rolling hills.

But there is nothing like cowtown,
The Trinity sublime.
Just plant me there near Fort Worth,
When it has come my time.

Cause God has blessed my Texas,
It don't take much to see.
The riches of his bounty,
They're good enough for me.

When Gabriel blows his trumpet,
He'll find my soul with ease.
Cause I'll be in God's country,
In Texas if you please.

Please Bury Me In Texas

Cowboys come from everywhere,
They call the range their home.
They work the trail from north to south,
Together and alone.

They often speak of where they're from,
As evening fires burn low.
Recalling things they want to share,
What they want you to know.

The talk it turns to girls and work,
Or horses they would own.
What they'll do when they get rich,
When they take their fortune home.

But as for me I ask one thing,
When I wrangle my last herd.
Just bury me in Texas,
Let that be my last word.

Cause God he has a cowboy's heart,
Just watch him play his hand.
He loves the sky, the range, the grass,
He's just an ole cowhand.

He made most waddies just like him,
Hard workers one and all.
Some is quiet and some is wild,
All are standing tall.

He loves Big Bend and Piney Woods,
The rolling plain is so vast.
The weather made by his own breath,
Great rivers running past.

From North to South he made it all,
Her beauty is her fame.
Oceans, mountains rolling hills,
The Llano western plains.

He gave this land a destiny,
In histories ever span.
Like no other place on earth,
He made her o' so grand.

God gave to us the best of all,
We're proud as we can be.
It's Texas that I call my home,
So there please bury me.

Cause when this drive is over,
With his tally book in hand.
He'll look for me in Texas,
Cause I carry his own brand.

Within The Arms Of God

We been through both thick and thin,
This ole horse and me.
We chased some cows and chased some
gals,
And shared some misery.

About last year as I recall,
At a rodeo out West.
Ole buck and me was in the hunt,
And we was at our best.

We made the cut a time or two,
But when the chips was down.
He couldn't make the final charge,
He slipped ... we both went down.

Now some I guess you'll blame on me,
Suppose that's just the luck.
But years of work and riding hard,
Had been real tough on Buck.

So when we fell in Billings,
I heard that muscle tear.
His heart was in the roping,
But his time was drawing near.

So yesterday at sun up,
With frost fresh on the ground.
I walked him to his favorite spot,
To put my old friend down.

I had to do what must be done,
His leg was torn and lame.
I think he saw it coming,
That just increased my pain.

His special place near waters edge,
With trees and grass galore.
I fed him one last sugar,
We talked of days of yore.

With eyes so full of tears for him,
I took the dreaded shot.
Within his heart he struggled,
But ... with little pain he dropped.

Now I know there's a heaven,
When old cowponies die.
Where they can act like colts again,
With water, grass and sky.

He'll nicker, buck, and paw the air,
Like in his younger years.
We'll meet again that horse and me,
Beyond these worldly tears.

I hope that he'll come running,
When he sees me at the gate.
As much as I will miss him,
Sometime I just can't wait.

I pray that God will welcome him,
To that pasture in the sky.
He's with the great remuda,
Where horses never die.

So there he lies my good ole friend,
Beneath the Texas sod.
Forever in my memories,
Within the arms of God.

*No man in the wrong can stand
up against a man in the right
who keeps on a coming*

Creed of the Texas Rangers

The Ringling Stage

The Ringling stage got robbed last night,
Near Cache Creek grade or so.
Three men were waiting in the trees,
When the team had stopped to blow.

With guns held high they called a halt,
With scarves across their face.
They blocked the road and stopped the
stage,
They picked the perfect place.

"Throw down that box," the leader said,
I'll never say it twice.
Curley did just what he said,
His eyes were cold as ice.

The leader swung his leg across,
His saddle to step down.
His spur hung in his slicker,
And his pony spun around.

Was bravery deep inside his soul,
Or dumb some folks would say.
But Curly grabbed the scatter gun,
And thus began the fray.

The 12 gauge bucked, let out a roar,
The leader fell stone dead.
Before he knew what hit him,
The next man lost his head.

The third man knew his time had come,
From there inside the coach.
Two forty-fives blazed lead and fire,
And he folded in the smoke.

The whole thing took 10 seconds,
The hands of time stood still.
Three men were dead the smoke was
cleared,
Out on that lonely hill.

It seems before it started,
The dreadful deed was done.
Three men who chose the bandit's life,
Had fallen to the gun.

So into town just down the road,
Their horses led in trail.
The gold and folks was safe aboard,
The stories they would tell.

So Curly standing at the bar,
Some farther down the line.
Said ... "I knowed the gold was
Butterfield's,
But the dang ole stage was mine."

Devil Horse

No one could ride that devil horse,
The stories went around.
He'd throw'd the best from east to west,
In many a frontier town.

Jet black was this wild Diablo,
With flowing mane and tail.
And most would swear this bag of hair,
Had come direct from hell.

They hauled him round from town to
town,
To test the skill and gall.
And many a cowboy bit the sand,
Some racked against the wall.

One hundred dollars Yankee gold,
If you can stay astride.
One minute on the wild black beast,
Ten dollars for your ride.

This day it dawned no different,
They lined up just to try.
And fifteen men from far and near,
Went sailing through the sky.

The last one came to try his hand,
The others laughed with glee.
A slight young man with freckled face,
Jumped from a nearby tree.

Into the ring this boy did step,
The crowd all drew a gasp.
He walked up to Diablo,
His mane he reached to grasp.

With head held high his eyes afire,
Diablo stepped away.
The boy reached out to stroke his neck,
He took a stand to stay.

Drawing ever closer,
He stroked the coat so black.
He whispered gently to the horse,
And slipped upon his back.

Now Diablo he just stood there,
The crowd was quiet as death.
You could see his nostrils ease and flare,
With each and every breath.

The satin skin it rippled,
He flinched and twitched his ear.
He pawed the sand and dipped his head,
The wranglers all stood clear.

What seemed to some eternal,
But moving in real time.
The boy he nudged the horses flanks,
To let him have his mind.

Then horse and boy rode round the ring,
They rode as one so proud.
A bond between the boy and horse,
To the cheering of the crowd.

Don't Judge A Horse By Its Looks

That rangy nag didn't look too tough,
When we cut her out to break.
Just like the rest, a bag o' bones,
That was our first mistake.

Her head she cocked it just a bit,
Her ears were pinned down flat.
If we was smart like we thought we was,
We'd a clued right in on that.

So we wrapped that rag across her eyes,
And laid that blanket on.
Ole Rich he slipped the bridle on,
She stood there like a stone.

When Harvey set the saddle on,
She quivered through and through.
Her nostrils flared, she gave a snort,
We never had a clue.

So far, so good, ole Dave climbed on,
We'd cinched that saddle tight.
But, that little mare was warming up,
She was plenty full of fight.

To our surprise she stood there,
Like she was fast asleep.
Then all at once she hit the sky,
Ten feet straight up at least.

She brought those hind legs past her
nose,
Her tail was like a whip.
Turned, bucked, pitched and then she
spun,
She gave ole Dave a nip.

She broke the gate that pinned her in,
The fence got damaged too.
Buckets, tack, and tools were flying,
She chased the whole darn crew.

The bunkhouse soon got in the way,
Through the door and out the side.
Ole Dave was flat as flat could be,
But he hung on through the ride.

She'd had enough the game was done,
That oak limb hung real low.
The saddle horn might clear the space,
But Dave would surely go.

She was on the other side,
Ole Dave was in the dirt.
That mare was headed out of sight,
For all that she was worth.

Except for saddle, tack and such,
We won't miss that bay.
It took two weeks to fix the place,
And cost us two months pay.

The lesson here is short and sweet,
I know you'll quickly learn.
Don't judge a horse by looks alone,
Most times you'll just get burned.

Yes....There is one great wrangler who owns the whole dang herd.

Texas Red

Be Careful Where You Race

Hot Dang! He said and slapped his knee,
A smile across his face.
A towhead kid and rangy nag,
Just won the Hoggtown race.

But not too fast, I'll get ahead,
There is a tale to share.
'Bout grub, and whiskey, horses fast,
And ladies oh so fair.

The Hoggtown race with highest stakes,
Brought men from miles around.
This year was no exception,
And their money filled the town.

Two riders seemed to set the mark,
Their mounts of fine bloodlines.
Bred to run from sun to sun,
And charge the finish line.

One lad was just a cowboy type,
From up near Spindle Top.
Long of mouth and short of brains,
He loved his chili hot.

The second was a fancy dude,
He wore a flat brimmed straw.
He bragged about his drinking skills,
And challenged one and all.

The other riders in the field,
Wouldn't draw a stare.
'Cept for that kid in patched up pants,
Who rode that rangy mare.

So eating and a drinking,
Was the order of the day.
Have some fun in Hoggtown,
The race was hours away.

On through the night they raised their
cane,
Never would they know.
That when the starter raised his gun,
Two riders wouldn't show.

A pretty lass a challenge made,
A neutral man would pour.
But she drank tea the dude drank rye,
Till he passed out on the floor.

The flat brimmed straw was bent and
torn,
The dude against the wall.
He'd lost his Hoggtown drinking bout,
He'd miss the starters call.

The cowboy on the doctor's bed,
Was doubled up with pain.
It must have been that chili hot,
He'd never eat again.

So bets were placed and odds were
struck,
New leaders filled their place.
Fifty-to-one on the kid and nag,
They lined up for the race.

Excitement filled the Hoggtown crowd,
As the horses took their mark.
The starter's gun was sounded,
Ten horses made the start.

The rangy nag with kid aboard,
Was holding with the pace.
Down by the creek around the turn,
Neck and neck they raced.

Then back behind the church yard,
The leaders thinning down.
The rangy mare was in the hunt,
As they started back to town.

They made the turn at Patton's mill,
Too many a startled face.
Then down through town across the line,
The kid had won the race.

He took the purse with sheepish smile,
As the dude was coming around.
A splitting head a busted hat,
He slipped on out of town.

The same thing for that cowboy,
His stomach still upset.
He mounted up and headed south,
And we ain't seen him yet.

43

They say he didn't go too far,
Just down the road from there.
He stopped to give the horse a drink,
And stroke his rangy mare.

He stroked the mare and mud came off,
Cool water did the trick.
A shiny coat of pure bloodlines,
Was under mud so thick.

The chili was homemade you know,
The kid's mom made the best.
She added in some special stuff,
The cowboy failed the test.

The pretty lass, his sister,
Who drank the dude to ground.
The neutral man an uncle,
Who poured the drinks all round.

So the moral to this little tale,
I'll tell you to your face.
Even with the best of skills,
Be careful where you race.

That Indian Kid

I never seen a rangy nag,
Throw such a wall-eyed fit.
Her fronts was in the stirrups,
Her backs were in the bits.

Ole Shorty must have bounced three
feet,
When he first hit the dirt.
That mare was spinning like a top,
Hell bent for all that she was worth.

She bucked them all that sunny day,
She throw'd the whole dang bunch.
No one was left to ride her,
When cookie rang for lunch.

The Indian kid dropped to the ground,
Been perched up on the fence.
He walked up to that bucking machine,
He didn't stand a chance.

But his approach was different,
The mare she seemed to know.
You could see her muscles quiver,
We're all waiting for the show.

That mare knew he was different,
Responding to his touch.
He stroked her neck and whither,
Slowly building trust.

He slipped the saddle off her,
He took the bridle too.
Replaced it with a hackamore,
Somehow that pony knew.

He didn't try to rush things,
Just gentle giving slack.
We all thought he was crazy,
When he slipped up on her back.

The boys all held their breath,
You couldn't hear a sound.
We waited for the action,
When that mustang quit the ground.

You know it never happened,
First right then left they'd go.
And out the gate he took that mare,
They galloped down the road.

They tell that story still today,
How the boys let out a cheer.
The day that lanky Indian kid,
Gentled down that wild-eyed mare.

Charlie Parkhurst,
Stage Coach Driver

Parkhurst was the Christian name,
Just Charlie to most all.
Hailed from up Rhode Island way,
And followed a westward call.

Came out west to make a name,
Drove stages to and fro.
Across the high Sierras,
Through dust and driving snow.

Was featured some in Harper's,
For manly looks so fine.
Cigar clinched between them teeth,
With six hitch team in line.

While many drivers worked the line,
They earned Wells-Fargo pay.
Some lived to tell and legend swelled,
Some filled an early grave.

But none were tougher to the core,
Who drove Wells-Fargo's load.
Than driver Charlie Parkhurst,
Hard weathered by the road.

O' many shared deep sadness,
When Charlie died one day.
A driver lost a legend gone,
As history passed away.

But as they laid him out to rest,
Right there before their eyes.
Ole Charlie was a woman,
His secret a surprise.

Cause through the years across the
miles,
Ole Charlie hauled the load.
All the time a woman,
And no one had ever knowed.

So men the world over,
A moral must be told ...
Just leave it to a woman,
To haul your mail and gold.

Just A Boy Of Ten
(The Gunfight at the OK Corral)

I seen it all the old man said,
Like it was yesterday.
From over there behind the barn,
Beside a stack of hay.

I was ten a towhead kid,
When that gunfight went down.
I was watching o'er the stock,
We'd just come into town.

I saw them coming down the street,
Well-heeled no sign of fear.
Determined in the task at hand,
As death drew ever near.

Down the street the cowboys stood,
Cock sure and full of fight.
They'd run their bluff this one more
time,
They'd raise some cane tonight.

Today it wasn't like the rest,
These men weren't like before.
They didn't scare, they didn't run,
They'd come to square the score.

Behind the badge they brought the law,
"Not so," some folks would say.
The cowboys thought they owned the
town,
Their time had come to pay.

So face-to-face the gunmen stood,
Not twenty feet apart.
Each waiting for the other,
This dance of death to start.

The Clantons and McLowerys,
Red sashes in the wind.
The Earps and Doctor Holiday,
Would face them man to man.

I don't know the first to fire,
Today it's hard to tell.
In less than sixty seconds,
Three men were sent to hell.

Two McLowerys and a Clanton,
Were lying cold and dead.
Doc took a minor hit,
Two Earps were hit with lead.

The total shots were thirty six,
Three men were cold and dead.
Ike and Billy ran like rats,
Like cowards so they said.

My account is straight and true,
From over near the barn.
Cause I was close and seen it all,
My story ain't no yarn.

October eighteen eighty-one,
Like it was yesterday.
The Earps and the cowboys had it out,
Three men a debt would pay.

50

The story wasn't over,
I'll tell another day.
How Wyatt and his "marshals,"
Made all the cowboys pay.

But now I'm old,
Most disregard some don't even care,
But that's the way I seen it done,
I know, cause I was there.

Choose friends slowly then stick to them through thick and thin.

Texas Red

You never saw an old cowpuncher.
They were scarce as hen's teeth.
Where they went to, heaven only knows.

John Clay
My Life on the Range

Common Sense

(The Words of Wyatt Earp)

Let's talk about the gunmen,
Their little dance with death.
Holiday and Masterson,
Could make you hold your breath.

Some little town it matters not,
The sun is at high noon.
Two men approach the street is clear,
One man will meet his doom.

The hand too quick for eyes to see,
The flash and then the roar.
A bullet streaks to find its mark,
A life will be no more.

Some say the edge goes to the man,
Who wears his hog leg low.
But some say high, some say cross,
And others just don't know.

But Wyatt shared the truth with all,
And history proved him right.
The man who brings the scatter gun,
Will always win the fight.

Nothing is easy except quitting.

Texas Red

Stage Coach West

Jump on board we're headed west,
The stage leaves town today.
Saint Louis bound for Frisco,
Three thousand miles away.

It won't take long to get there,
Just twenty-four days and nights.
Through dust and rain, mud and snow,
Delays and Injun fights.

That Concord coach rides nice and
smooth,
The best stage man could make.
Unless the road is washed away by rain,
Somewhere along the way.

The food you'll eat comes extra,
For a dollar maybe two.
It's something you'll remember,
That great slumgullion stew.

There's room aboard for everyone,
Fifteen inches for your seat.
It's something you'll get use to,
With your luggage round your feet.

The price is right to make the trek,
Three hundred dollars gold.
There's dirt and heat in summer time,
And winters' freezing cold.

The lodging all along the route,
Will leave you wanting more.
The drivers get what beds there is,
The riders get the floor.

Swing stations give a change of stock,
Each dozen miles or so.
Home stations get you meals and such,
As westward on you go.

There's Indians waiting for you,
Along the whole dang road.
Some is tame and some is not,
And some you just don't know.

You'll need some blankets for the cold,
For sure don't grease your hair.
Watch your tongue with ladies near,
Don't let them hear you swear.

Twenty-five pounds is all you take,
So pack with extra care.
Just pants and shirts and basic stuff,
You'll need it way out there.

So take a slug and chew a plug,
Be careful where you spit.
I would advise some caution too,
In where you choose to sit.

So God bless Mr. Butterfield,
His first class ride out west.
He had the only game in town,
Therefore, it was the best.

When you get to California,
You've jerked near every bone.
I believe you'll take the Steam Boat,
When you're headed back to home.

Wishing don't make it so.

Texas Red

*In April, 1874, on Hell
Roaring Creek in the Indian
Territory, two outfits had their
entire remudas frozen to death
in a night of wind-driven snow
and sleet. One outfit lost
seventy-eight horses.*

*Wayne Gard
The Chisholm Trail*

Crossing Of The Red

I've heard them tell those stories,
So many times they said.
The trail is rough, but nothing tough,
Like crossing of the Red.

We started north that fine spring day,
With about three thousand head.
With chuck, remuda, crew of twelve,
All heading for the Red.

The trail was fresh, the grass was sweet,
The streams were none to dread.
Just streams with limestone bottoms,
And nothing like the Red.

We crossed the herd at Austin,
The Colorado coming down.
We watered them at Waco,
Swam the Brazos east of Town.

The Trinity just lay there,
Her bed just north of town.
No rain to cause a problem,
But thunder all around.

We saw the clouds out west of us,
A hundred miles ahead.
It rained for days 'til Denton,
As we approached the Red.

Now the little streams were running
high,
But we never lost a head.
We knew the worst was coming,
With the crossing of the Red.

The boss rode out upon a rise,
To take a look with dread.
He told us not to rush the herd,
We'd be holding at the Red.

Them clouds that we'd been watching,
Dropped rain way up ahead.
And rim to rim she's running wild,
There'd be no crossing of the Red.

So hold 'em at the station,
With the river running high.
Too thick to drink, too thin to plow,
With rumbling in the sky.

That river's like a woman,
Flowing sweet and slow.
Then like a flash of lightening,
She lets her fury go.

Now boss he knew the dangers,
As he watched the mighty Red.
Quicksand, trees and whirlpools,
Left many a waddie dead.

So we settled down to camp chores,
To tasks we'd left undone.
We visited at the station,
Played cards and had some fun.

And then one morning early,
The boss rode to the rim.
That lady she had settled down,
Back in her bed again.

We moved the herd down slowly,
Red water swirling round.
Horns and nose bout all to see,
We prayed they wouldn't drown.

By noon we made the crossing,
We did lose twenty head.
The worst was now behind us,
We had crossed the mighty Red.

The man who wins the gun fight brings a sawed off shotgun.

Wyatt Earp

The Fall Of 81

You've heard the tales from north to
south,
'Bout cowboys and hip wear.
Well, I am here to set you straight,
The truth you're gonna hear.

I'll tell of Wyatt and Virg and Morg,
The brothers Earp and friends.
The McLowerys and the Clantons,
And how they met their end.

Romancers and slick sayers,
Their fancy stories weave.
And dime store novels one and all,
Don't care who they deceive.

But John P. Clum the Editor,
Put all of this to pen.
Recorded in the Epitaph,
How these outlaws met their end.

The fued had long been comin,
The trouble we know well.
A fight had been a making,
That would send some men to hell.

The Clantons and McLowerys,
And Billy Claiborne too.
A gang made up by Curly Bill,
In their forty dollar boots.

The other side, the brothers Earp,
All badged and sworn to law.
Were pushed to fight and make their
play,
Their pride against the wall.

The ringer in this shooting spree,
Is something I must say.
He lived with death on every breath,
The Doctor Holiday.

In late October 81,
The feud came to a head.
OK Corral in Tombstone town,
Three cowboys lying dead.

No western romance could be found,
With guns and blazing lead.
Frank took a shot right to his heart,
A second through his head.

Ike Clanton wouldn't jerk his gun,
He ran down Allen Street.
His brother Billy met his fate,
At Morg and Virgil's feet.

The air went still, the fight was done,
Three dozen shots had flown.
Three men were hit, three more were
dead,
And Wyatt stood alone.

Seconds only timed the fight,
Too fast for most to see.
But Tombstone and this ole horse corral,
Still lives in History.

(Footnote)

The Cowboys with their sashes red,
Would strike within the night.
They did their best on Virg and Morg,
But wouldn't stand and fight.

So in the end as you will see,
As history was to tell.
Wyatt took the law in hand,
And sent the rest to hell.

Friends are few, real friends are almost never.

Texas Red

"To rise up from a man's table and war upon that man while the taste of his bread is still sweet in your mouth-such dealings would have been unspeakable infamy....You must not smile and shoot."

Gene Rhodes
Cowboy Ethics

Ole Red On Ice

Ole Red he's just a lying there,
His Sunday shirt and pants.
His stash is waxed his hair slicked back,
Like he was in a trance.

The smithy made a nice pine box,
And Red looks so darned nice.
The problem is it's summer,
And we're running out of ice.

A few months hence if he been throwed,
The problem ain't so great.
It's a hundred and ten in the summer
shade,
And his funeral just can't wait.

If it was last December,
We'd have lots of ice.
We'd take our time and have a wake,
With fixings o' so nice.

There'd be food and stories told,
And all his friends would come.
But ice is scarce and weather's hot,
And business must be done.

You gotta play the hand you're dealt,
No time for funerals grand.
Plant him now up on the hill,
Ole red would understand.

We'll have to choose the shorter course,
It's hot this time of year.
Two things will help us make our choice,
It's Red or ice cold beer.

So in the ground ole Red will go,
We'll drink a toast all round.
We'll ice the beer and bury Red,
With friends that can be found.

We'll place him in his resting place,
Six feet beneath the ground.
Cold beer we'll have instead of Red,
We'll drink his health all round.

The Mighty Chisholm Trail

The Chisholm Trail runs only north,
From deep in Texas' soul.
Ten million head of Longhorns pushed,
By waddies young and bold.

O'er twenty years we'll give or take,
The trail served many well.
From livelihoods to the dinner plate,
The stories it could tell.

About young boys grown up to be men,
Some left along the way.
Great men and ranches made and lost,
Some with us still today.

Some heroes lived this history,
But most were common men.
Who pushed the herds to rail head
towns,
Then home to start again.

A nation fed with Texas beef,
The Longhorn's claim to fame.
Shipped by rail to markets east,
And stocked the northern plains.

Most markers lost to times strong hand,
But others still remain.
Like crossing of the mighty Red,
Landmarks upon the plains.

While highways might well cross the
land,
The plans will never change.
Those routes picked out by foremen,
For water, grass, and range.

If those who have a cowboy heart,
Share stories, poems, and tales.
Forever will the legend live,
Of the mighty Chisholm trail.

That's What A Cowboy'd Say

When shadows stretch across the plain,
And the sun is glowing red.
Cookie's got the coals banked up,
The horses have been fed.

The trail day's long like most before,
The sky turns rusty brown.
The herd is milling peacefully,
Nightriders start their rounds.

But clouds are building in the west,
A halo's round the moon.
The seasons right for thunderstorms,
You hear their distant booms.

One grazing steer perks up his ear,
He hears the rolling sound.
The wind picks up and whips the grass,
We dread that moaning sound.

Now clouds have banked across the
moon,
A drizzle starts to fall.
The temperature has dropped a notch,
The cattle start to bawl.

Then from the gray and rolling clouds,
The lightning starts to flash.
We're up and in our slickers,
And to the herd we dash.

The lightning splits the cold black air,
The thunder rips the night.
The first cow blots, then two, then three,
The whole herd moves in fright.

Then all at once the herd is up,
In mass they charge in fright.
The riders rush to gain the lead,
Just shadows in the night.

Nothing stops this dangerous dance,
Not horse, nor rope, nor gun.
Till they chase fear out from their eyes,
You gotta let them run.

They race across the open plain,
Through brush and grass they churn.
With cowboys riding for the lead,
The monsters head to turn.

At breakneck speed they run headlong,
Through rain and lighting flash.
Nothing seems to slow their race,
In their devil's driven dash.

Sure footed ponies, fearless men,
They finally gain control.
They've run ten miles and maybe more,
No telling what the toll.

Like a wave that's hit the shore,
Their fury all is spent.
They settle down and mill around,
Gentle and content.

All night long we guard the herd,
The storm moves on away.
We'll check the price we had to pay,
First thing at break of day.

It's just a part of this dang job,
It's just another day.
It's forty and found most every month,
That's what a Cowboy'd say.

If something don't kill you, it'll make you stronger.

Texas Red

The Dime Novel

I just guess I never knew,
How glamorous we are.
Til I read it in a little book,
At Grafton's general store

Cowboys ride to setting sun,
Pausing on a hill.
To bond with nature just one time,
And share the north wind chill.

We sing to doggies every night,
To ease their troubled mind.
To make them feel so cozy,
While freezing our behind.

We close in round the camp fire,
As evening settles low.
To eat and share our stories,
All gathered in the snow.

Our trusty mount beneath us,
We share our everyday.
We close our bond of friendship,
While pitching loads of hay.

Awake at dawn we greet the day,
A smile is on our face.
So coffee stout, and biscuits hot,
The dust blows cross our plate.

But gathered round the bunk house,
A guitar on our knee.
We sing a song and write to home,
And share our bed with fleas.

Our dress is so romantic,
Our costume always new.
Silken scarves and Stetson hats,
My boots is worn plumb through.

Life is good, the air is fresh,
They don't mean to brag.
The range is free, the sky is clear,
Especially riding drag.

I guess them novels all is true,
The stories right in line.
Just what a person ought to get,
If they only pay a dime.

Shorty And The Fight

Sometimes when dinner time is done,
The coffee tastes just right.
Talk will turn to times gone past,
To Shorty and the fight.

Seems that Shorty went to town,
And stopped in for a beer.
He asked a gal to dance with him,
And the story starts right here.

Some cowboys from the XIT,
Said, Hey that gal is mine.
Shorty he just stepped on back,
Said please excuse, that's fine.

The cowboy had his dander up,
Some say as mad as hell.
Shorty turned to walk away,
And wished the young girl well.

Not good enough, the cowboy said,
Apologize to me.
Shorty turned and touched his hat,
As nice as he could be.

See Shorty he was five foot six,
Not much of him to fear.
His arms were large his hands were too,
His eyes were blue and clear.

I don't fight ole Shorty said,
Just come to have some fun.
If this here gal is spoken for,
She ain't the only one.

I'm just here to play some cards,
To have a beer tonight.
No need to take this personal,
Ain't looking for a fight.

The cowpoke he was plumb wound up,
He stood near six feet two.
His ego pushed his brains aside,
He'd whip the whole dang crew.

No words would make this kid unwind,
He let the liquor talk.
We'll go out back to settle this,
We'll take a little walk.

They went out back to clear the slate,
This slight to reconcile.
The cowboy feeling in his prime,
While Shorty hid a smile.

Before he joined the cowboy life,
He'd had a famous name.
The square ring was his place of work,
And boxing was his game.

They say he never lost a round,
In fifty fights or more.
Big and small he took them all,
He'd laid them on the floor.

Back home he fought for money,
Came west to work the range.
Once called the New York Hammer,
Out here he changed his name.

Let's take off our boots and spurs,
That way we'll keep it fair.
Don't you gouge and I won't bite,
We'll stay inside this square.

The cowboy did as Shorty said,
He gave his fighter look.
Then Shorty hit him with a right,
And crossed it with a hook.

Out cold as clay the cowboy went,
Before he hit the ground.
So back inside to drink and dance,
And Shorty bought the round.

A little morale if you will,
Go have yourself some fun.
But share with all that dance hall girl,
She ain't the only one.

If you fight to win, don't stop till you've won.

Texas Red

The Llano Estacado

It goes so far there ain't no end,
Touched by the hand of God.
No fence to block a moving herd,
No plows had turned the sod.

It's the Llano Estacado,
The Spanish gave the name.
Where buffalo and Indians roamed,
Before the white man came.

Much history has been written here,
Across this great plateau.
By cowboys and by soldiers,
And some we'll never know.

The greatest of the ranches,
The mighty XIT.
Stretched out two days in every way,
The grandest sight to see.

Most Texas rivers start there,
The Brazos and the Red.
Through the Texas heartland,
The mighty state is feed.

Sacred are the canyons,
The red men sang their praise.
The soldiers used the Thule,
For a thousand ponies graves.

The Alibates you'll find up north,
Spread across this wondrous land.
They traded wide this special flint,
With many an Indian band.

Adobe walls still beckons all,
Who trace out times own sand.
Where Quanta and his band of braves,
Fought for one last stand.

A thousand yards the shot was made,
Though some still call it luck.
But Dixon gets the credit,
He killed that Indian buck.

Mckinze, Loving, Goodnight,
Are names of legend there.
The Slaughters and brothers Mooar,
This special place still share.

So when you see a lonely hawk,
Above this wondrous plain.
Remember that the face has changed,
But the spirits still remain.

Look Out Dodge City

When I get off this trail Drive,
This herd is in the pens.
We're gonna rip the top off Dodge,
Raise cane from end-to-end.

We best not cross the deadline,
The law will knock you flat.
There ain't no need to push your luck,
There's no fun north of that.

We'll get some pay to start our spree,
A bath and shave to start.
Some duckins and a brand new shirt,
We'll start out looking smart.

Might just buy a brand new scarf,
A Stetson for a crown.
Get measured for a pair of boots,
If time allows in town.

No telling just how good we'll look,
We'll drop our spurs a notch.
We'll amble down them ole boardwalks,
To give them girls a shock.

We'll take the gin mills one-by-one,
Like soldiers on campaign.
We'll dance and drink and have some
fun,
'Til we don't feel no pain.

Sometime we might get rowdy,
Our fun sometimes is loud.
But we don't mean to do no harm,
Just Texans feeling proud.

It seems somehow it never fails,
Some time real late at night.
Two waddies want the same darn gal,
Some cowboy starts a fight.

They don't know it ain't true love,
She tells them all the same.
Spends your pay on rot gut rye,
That's how she plays the game.

Before it's done I'll guarantee,
You'll have a tale to tell.
The Marshall or his deputy,
Will throw your butt in jail.

Free room and board will be your lot,
The judge will set your bail.
Half your pay and an aching head,
Will be your tale to tell.

Then back to camp no jingle left,
We'll leave ole Dodge behind.
We're headed south for Texas,
We'll do it right next time.

Rolling Smokes

Did you ever try to roll a smoke,
While working on the range.
The wind is blowing ninety plus,
And it drives you plumb insane.

Your leg across the saddle horn,
Your backside to the wind.
You shake it out, then whiff it's gone,
And then you try again.

There's nothing to it at the ranch,
Or near the cookie's fly.
But try it on the open range,
And kiss your smoke goodbye.

Cause when you get the paper rolled,
The Durham laid so right.
You start to lick and oops it's gone,
The darned ole thing takes flight.

So take your fixins out again,
And give one more a try.
You gotta have a darned ole smoke,
Or you'll most likely die.

Your fingers make the perfect roll,
Dab them fixins in.
Hold your breath and start to lick,
Here comes that doggone wind.

But finely on the fifth time,
You get that smoke rolled tight.
Between your lips now get a match,
And the wind blows out your light.

The Last Game

Don't draw that gun the stranger said,
Let's don't make a fight.
I just came to play some cards,
Don't want to take your life.

He slipped the leather thong aside,
To let he hammer clear.
Again he warned the cowboy,
Let's stop this thing right here.

How many times this thing he'd seen,
This tragic race he'd run.
A cowboy who had lost at cards,
Would settle with his gun.

This time it might be different,
He didn't think it so.
'Cause cowboys never were too fast,
Their draw was way too slow.

Though earnest were their efforts,
Bullheaded with a flair.
They lived their lives fullspeed ahead,
And seldom had a care.

He'd seen it in the railheads,
Dodge City and the like.
Sometimes a girl, sometimes a drink,
They'd somehow want to fight.

But he had let his focus slip,
A momentary lapse.
His drifting back to times gone by,
Could be a fatal trap.

The barmaid had been pushed aside,
The boy jumped to his feet.
Slow motion seemed to frame the scene,
No voices heard to speak.

From his hand the cards askew,
He reeled back from in his chair.
His hand went down to find his gun,
His first shots filled the air.

He took a roll across the floor,
His Colt was now in place.
The cowboy shot a second time,
And splinters hit his face.

But noise and blood would not prevail,
This cowboy shot his last.
Three shots rang out and found their
mark,
As from this world he passed.

The gun fell from the cowboy's hand,
The other grabbed the wound.
The crowd in time was frozen,
And smoke now filled the room.

The barmaid tried to break his fall,
His weight she couldn't bear.
She crouched so close beside him,
His dying words to hear.

Though self-defense the motive,
The stranger knew the score.
He swept the money from the game,
And headed for the door.

Escape was not to be his fate,
This game had been his last.
The law was waiting in the street,
He never heard the blast.

Remember that dance hall girls work for the house.

𝒯𝑒𝓍𝒶𝓈 𝑅𝑒𝒹

The dealer always has the edge.

𝒯𝑒𝓍𝒶𝓈 𝑅𝑒𝒹

The Coming Of The Wire

Seventy One as I recall,
The ole man took a chew.
The first time that I seen the wire,
I know'd the range was through.

He put his hands behind his neck,
Leaned back in that ole chair.
He told me things about the West,
When he was young with flare.

The range was open north and south,
As far as you could go.
From Mexico to Canada,
I guess I ought to know.

We drove them cows by thousands,
Them rangy Longhorn steers.
To railheads up in Kansas,
For brands long gone by years.

You know I seen it coming,
Up on the XIT.
100 miles of stretched barbed wire,
As far as you could see.

They cut the range across the trail,
With wire and post and such,
Some fought it with their cutters,
It didn't slow down much.

It kept the farmers crops all safe,
From cows once ranging free.
No prairie grass forever now,
Like once it used to be.

Some say it's good, some say not,
I guess I just don't know.
I finished up a riding fence,
And that's just how it goes.

"Alambre, alambre! Alambre! todas partes!" ("Wire! wire! wire! everywhere!") Barbed wire had so changed the lay of the land in the Indian's eyes that even they were confused on how to get back home to Taos.

Spoken to Charles Goodnight by a Pueblo chief in the panhandle of Texas in the late 1870s

The Slicker With The Mouth

I hear the gavel sounding,
As clear as yesterday.
We stayed two extra nights in Dodge,
With our pockets full of pay.

We didn't really mean no harm,
Just looking for some fun.
But they kinda took it personal,
When they seen the stuff we done.

So here we stand before the judge,
He ain't a happy man.
And over there a deputy,
With the shotgun in his hand.

We didn't know that slicker,
Was the Mayor's son-in-law.
Or we'd just tipped our hats to him,
There'd never been a brawl.

He said some things about our looks,
We could have let it go.
But when he laughed at Texas,
Ole Curley laid him low.

Ole Curley he's most muscle,
From down near old Round Rock.
But he sure got his dander up,
And he gave that boy a pop!

You might expect that was the end,
But that was not to be.
Cause there was two, then four, and
more,
We really had a spree.

The whole dang room was in the fray,
Just boots and teeth and gore.
I took a lick and down I went,
Woke up upon the floor.

I do recall that shotgun blast,
The local law arrived.
From where I sit I guess I'm glad,
At least I'm still alive.

How that lawman broke his jaw,
I'll bet that really hurt?
His mangled ear and bloodshot eye,
That sleeve tore off his shirt.

That deputy with the broken arm,
Will mend as good as new.
It must have been an act of God,
As through that door he flew.

Them teeth marks on the barkeep's
back,
Just how did they get there.
That bandage there across his head,
Where yesterday was hair.

That busted lip with front tooth gone,
It makes an ugly sight.
We was meek as church mice,
We never came to fight.

About this time the Judge turned red,
He'd heard it all ... Enough!
He cleared his throat sat up real
straight,
And yelled at me ... SHUT UP!

He said, "I've heard enough from you,
You're guilty sure as sin.
I'll sure get your attention,
Should you visit Dodge again.

One hundred dollars from each man,
All damages you'll pay.
I suggest you fork your mounts,
And get along your way."

So two months pay right down a hole,
And we're all headed south.
We're headed back to Texas,
But we shut that slicker's mouth.

A mouth don't make a man.

Texas Red

The Wiry Kid

He weren't much, just a wiry kid,
Most bone and hair and skin.
Ridden hard and put up wet,
The night that he rode in.

Didn't have too much to say,
But ate them beans right down.
He hadn't eat in quite a while,
We was way outside of town.

The cookie had a blanket,
A slicker came from Red.
A hat came flying through the air,
Nothing much was said.

He looked to me 'bout ten or twelve,
Was tall to be that age.
Hands were rough but eyes were soft,
His heart seemed filled with rage.

The foreman kind of liked him,
Most likely saw himself.
Early the next morning,
He cut him out a mount.

Told him to help the cookie,
Watch the horses and ride drag.
He ate that dust enough to choke,
Would make a grown man gag.

He worked at every job he got,
One never to complain.
But sadness registered in this boy,
Each manjack shared his pain.

Then shortly after dinner,
The herd was still and quiet.
He stood and thanked us one and all,
Then talked on through the night.

Times was tough and he was young,
His real paw left their home.
His new paw didn't like him,
He took off on his own

His horse had only pulled a plow,
And had never pushed a cow.
He expected he could find some work,
He'd learn a trade somehow.   .

He really didn't have much luck,
No work for kids like him.
Until he saw ole cookie's fire,
That night we took him in.

He thanked us for our kindness,
To help him get a start.
He asked if he could stay around,
He went straight to our heart.

Well that darn kid worked day and night,
He never missed a call.
He learned to brand, to rope, to ride,
He dang near learned it all.

Now years have passed, this boy is gone,
He's working as top hand.
Riding tall not looking back,
This boy has made a hand.

Never try a bluff that you can't back up.

Texas Red

"Few more wild, reckless scenes of abandoned debauchery can be seen on the civilized earth than a dance house in full blast in one of the frontier towns."

Joe McCoy
Rancher

It's Winter At The Ranch

It won't be long, the ducks are gone,
The trees are standing bare.
Each morning now the air is crisp,
And winter's in the air.

The boss has let some waddies go,
It happens every year.
The grubline just a way of life,
And some just disappear.

We're just enough to play a hand,
In the bunkhouse every night.
But work is slow and we all know,
The money's getting tight.

The wood's laid in, the hay's been
stacked,
The line shake men are gone.
The days are short, we see some frost,
The nights are getting long.

I guess I'll need to get to town,
My slicker's four years old.
I'll need that thing to cut the wind,
And stop the winter cold.

I've seen the snow get belly deep,
On a mare at 18 hands.
While riding fence some years ago,
Upon another brand.

Ole man winter really howled that year,
    I nearly lost my way.
I purt near froze myself to death,
    If it wasn't for that bay.

She had nose for finding home,
She showed it late that night.
We made it to that line shack,
As morning broke first light.

It's mending tack and marking time,
    Cards and games of chance.
It's me and Lou and Texas Red,
    Doing winter on the ranch.

Changing Of The West

It's hard to think they're mostly gone,
It seems like yesterday.
The greatest brands, the open range,
Like ashes drift away.

The XIT in Texas,
The largest anywhere.
A hundred miles of open range,
Was large beyond compare.

The JA, Charlie Goodnight's spread,
Fell to the hands of time.
Where Loving and the Colonel,
Worked cattle in their prime.

Ole Pastor Slaughter and his boys,
Drove up the Chisholm Trail.
The range is gone but legends live,
In stories that we tell.

The Flying V, the Matador,
The town still bears that name.
Out in Motley County,
Most gone but some remain.

Great ranches like some men live on,
Some in a cowboy's mind.
Like memories they will linger,
Until the end of time.

Yet some still live and hold their ground,
The legends seem to last.
They run their cows and horses,
Like ages that have past.

The King ranch running W,
Down on the coastal plain.
Now world-wide and much revered,
By change they've been maintained.

Four Sixes out near Guthrie,
Like Captain Burk was there.
Still running stock like years gone past,
There's history everywhere.

The Pitchfork in West Texas,
If you care to make the drive.
The Croton Breaks ain't changed a lot,
Keeps cowboy life alive.

They drove the beef to markets east,
They stocked the northern plain.
Swing EZ, Square, and Compass,
The Wine Cup I can name.

Snake River and the Elkhorn,
Ran longhorn cattle too.
The Circle Dot, A-up-A Down,
If stories are all true.

It's just a few that we know well,
There's others I could name.
Some linger on in pieces,
But their grandeur ain't the same.

There was a time when cowboys young,
They rode the biggest brand.
They pushed them cows a thousand
miles,
Across this open land.

But most is gone yet some remain,
When man was at his best.
History left them in the past,
Just the changing of the West.

When all is said and done,
what you leave behind is who
you were...not what you did.
Reputation takes a lifetime to
build and one lie to destroy.

Texas Red

Who Really Won The West

Most folks out west were mighty tough,
  They worked to make their way.
Some pushed a plow, some pushed a
  cow,
  Or worked in town for pay.

But stories go and legends grow,
  'Bout men with outlaw ways.
Who lived their life out on the edge,
  Until their dying day.

History often paints these men,
  A product of their time.
They turned to guns and outlaw gangs,
  To live a life of crime.

Their lives grew hard as gun blue steel,
  Their sleep a fitful rest.
Living high when times were good,
  But none would stand the test.

Banks and trains were targets rich,
  For men with nerves and skill.
But living fast and running hard,
  Got many an outlaw killed.

No need to name them one by one,
  Their stories end the same.
A boot hill cross or just a hole,
  No marker for their name.

But stories go and legends grow,
About this worthless lot.
They shoot good men and raped the
land,
'Til most of them were shot.

But truth be known this land was
grown,
By men without a gun.
They pushed a plow or pushed a cow,
And worked from sun to sun.

They left their mark with sweat and dirt,
Not death or crime like some.
We owe to them a debt of thanks,
For all the work they've done.

No legends grown or wild seeds sown,
Stand up to times tough test.
Twas visions clear and plain hard work,
That really won the West.

Saddle'n up Time

Was it yesterday or was it years ago,
We were in our prime.
Just like young pups so full of pep,
Each day at saddle'n up time.

The air was crisp, the sky was clear,
The east a silver glow.
Excitement filled that magic time,
The ponies seemed to know.

On winter's cold and frosty morn,
Through Spring and Summer's fine.
How I love the smell of sage,
Each day at saddle'n up time.

Some was quiet, some full of talk,
As tack and horse combined.
All though about the work ahead,
Each day at saddle'n up time.

Before the sun broke free of earth,
We're saddled up and gone.
Headed for the daily tasks,
By teams or some alone.

I love the time that's in-between,
God's wonder is so fine.
We see it every day at dawn,
We're here at saddle'n up time.

It didn't matter what the job,
When we were in our prime.
The days was laid out one by one,
Each day at saddle'n up time.

We spent our youth with cows and
friends,
Upon the open range.
We seldom thought beyond the day,
No fear that things might change.

But, Shorty he got throwed last year,
It hurt him really bad.
And Billy took a job in town,
A working for his dad.

We found ole Lefty in a drift,
Last spring on higher range.
And Sam just up and quit the crew,
His leaving seemed real strange.

I know I'm getting older,
I look around and see.
The hands are all much younger,
And fewer look like me.

They probably think I'm too darn old,
I feel I'm well broke in.
I'll do another round up,
And beat the best of them.

I've seen a lot of trail drives,
Don't feel that I'm near through.
Been up the Chisholm once or twice,
The Goodnight Loving too.

110

My heart and mind say I'm O.K.,
I think I'm doing fine.
I'll pull my weight and maybe more,
Each day at saddle'n up time.

Someday I know I'll cash it in,
I hope my time ain't near.
I want to reach that upper range,
With my tally book all clear.

I'll meet the greatest wrangler,
Who keeps this world in line.
Till then I guess I'll look ahead,
To one more saddle'n up time.

"Texas is the only place in the world where you can stand knee deep in mud and the dust will blow in your face at forty below zero."

Texas Red

A pocket full of pay makes a lot of friends.

Texas Red

All railhead women love you more than the last cowboy.

Texas Red

Memorial Hill

If you sit here like I have done,
I think you'll feel the lure.
A place like this will stir your soul,
Of times gone past before.

You cross the Red and head them north,
The IT next to face.
The plain spreads out before you,
This is a wondrous place.

It isn't much to look at,
A rise above the plain.
Some miles beyond The Spanish Fort,
Memorial Rock by name.

But when you sit upon the top,
The view is broad and grand.
Where foremen rolled a smoke to rest,
Upon this sacred land.

It sits along the Chisholm Trail,
Where the cattle slowly trod.
Northward up to Kansas,
To Ellsworth or to Dodge.

Ten thousand head they say you'd see,
From north to south they spread.
Just some of millions passing by,
To keep this country fed.

So while the trail has grown new grass,
Its marks are lost to time.
Some cowboy carved his ranches brand,
And left his mark behind.

Along this Longhorn highway,
There's no place quite as fine.
Where the trail rolls out before you,
And stops the hands of time.

So sit upon this windswept hill,
And let your soul take stock.
You'll see them cows and waddies all,
From high atop that rock.

Would You Believe?

I know you've heard of railhead towns,
  Of herds and cowboy crews.
  But most of that is fiction,
  I'm here to spread the truth.

Why, cows is smart and clever too,
  They'd make a perfect pet.
  Most ain't had no chance at all,
  To prove their worth as yet.

Their nature is so very kind,
  They're quick to make a friend.
  Why, we could learn a thing or two,
  If we'd just study them.

And dance hall girls has got a rap,
  Just meanness I'd suspect.
  They is really angels,
  Pure hearts is my best guess.

Some say they drink cheap rye and beer,
  And dance the whole night through.
  Except some nights they stay up late,
  To study Sunday school.

When we hit town with four months pay,
  We pass our time with care.
  The Christian Science reading room,
  You'll find the whole crew there.

We stay as meek as church mice,
Share quite time by the hour.
Or stop down by the church house,
To practice with the choir.

The old folks like to see us,
They know we'll visit them.
We carry food and do some chores,
And help the ones shut-in.

When we gather after dark,
For sporting and some fun.
We tip our hats and act our best,
And never shoot our guns.

The sheriff is glad to see us too,
He speaks with fondest tones.
He knows we're all just lonely boys,
So far away from home.

Before we leave his friendly town,
I'll bet he'll come to call.
We're such a warm and friendly bunch,
He'll want to know us all.

So when you hear those railhead tales,
You've heard the truth from me.
Cowboys far away from home,
Is sweet as they can be.

The Lacey Hat

We was headed back from town,
It was just the other day.
Was me and Fred and them two mules,
Just easing on our way.

The list was long we had to fill,
The monthly groceries too.
Special things for everyone,
Some orders from the crew.

We had that buckboard loaded up,
All tied so neat and tight.
Coffee, flour, and wire and such,
And a hat for the foreman's wife.

Now once we got her loaded up,
We was dry as two bleached bones.
We had a beer at Logan's bar,
Then headed out for home.

We started out 'bout sundown,
Just dawdling down the road.
The mules was pulling steady,
Despite the heavy load.

We'd gone along about ten miles,
Was most near sound asleep.
So we never seen it coming,
There was not a single peep.

I just don't know what spooked them
mules,
A rabbit or a snake.
But something scared them near to
death,
And they headed out of state.

Ole Fred he woke too late to act,
We was flying down the road.
Their ears pinned back in total fear,
Thank God we tied that load.

But, then, them mules broke off the road,
Across the open range.
Hell bent, bug-eyed and running wild,
Two animals insane.

That rig was riding on two wheels,
Them mules changed end for end.
We hung on half-near scared to death,
Then they pulled that move again.

We hit a log that no one saw,
The buckboard took a jerk.
The tie-down broke and stuff flew loose,
There went all our work.

I seen that hat go flying out,
With wire and coffee too.
Flour bags and sugar sacks,
We knew that load was through.

So across the plain this wagon went,
Spreading out the load.
About five miles by my best guess,
We couldn't see the road.

Ole Fred he got them simmered down,
He pulled them reins up tight.
Too late to save that load of freight,
We left an awful sight.

Cause stretched out-cross that open
plain,
Was our buckboard full of stuff.
There's bags and sacks and odds and
ends,
It all looked pretty rough.

To think a bunny or a snake,
Could cause this kind of mess.
And spread this stuff both far and wide,
Across the great Southwest.

So 'bout mid-night we made'er home,
We picked up all we could.
Most was saved but some was lost,
And some was no dang good.

We even found that lacey hat,
For the foreman's waiting wife.
That other stuff we could have lost,
But that hat would have cost our life.

Wish on one hand and spit in the other...which one fills up fastest ?

Texas Red

Nature's Church

There weren't too many churches,
On the frontier in the West.
But folks they gathered anyway,
For God to have them blessed.

The farther that you got out West,
The fewer folks called home.
Almost nothing out there,
But some folks there would roam.

It didn't take no wood or paint,
No pews or steeple bell.
Everywhere that folks would come,
Their God was there as well.

No ceiling but the rolling clouds,
No stained glass but the sky.
The music was the whispering wind,
Through grass it rustled by.

At night the stars shown high above,
The moon shown like a flame.
It brought a glow with God's own touch,
Across the Llano's plain.

The red man knew this holy shrine,
For time too long to tell.
He knew of nature's temple,
It served him oh so well.

He watched the sun rise on the plains,
A golden glowing orb.
Just like it did so long ago,
To herald Easter morn.

He never built his churches tall,
Obstructing nature's view.
No organs sounded greatly,
He never saw a pew.

So who was closest to their God?
Where gold and glass abound?
Or native souls on Texas plains,
Where God is all around.

He Was Just A Cowboy

He was just a Cowboy,
No more for me to say.
Young and full of vinegar,
He passed along our way.

He was just a Cowboy,
He worked hard for his pay.
Had nothing when he started,
And left this life that way.

He was just a Cowboy,
He drove the Chisholm Trail.
Pushed cows up north to Abilene,
And lived to tell the tale.

He was just a Cowboy,
Rode drag when he was young.
Branded, broke, and rode some fence,
And loved to have his fun.

He was just a Cowboy,
He didn't like to walk.
Rode his horse most everywhere,
And was skimpy with his talk.

He was just a Cowboy,
He rode the open range.
The spreads he knew them one and all,
Their brands and foreman's name.

He was just a Cowboy,
Few worldly goods he owned.
His tack, his boots, a worn-out gun,
Some letters from back home.

He was just a Cowboy,
What more is there to say?
He put things into motion.
His legend lives today.

Ashes In The Wind

When I look back I plainly see,
My life in blocks of time.
Some things seem so important,
But what is left behind?

We're like the range once open wide,
Now crossed with roads and fence.
And endless sea, the Llano,
Like we'll never see again.

Once traveled by the buffalo,
First north then south again.
Their movement by the weather,
They ranged from end to end.

He saw it climbing from the west,
His home came quick to mind.
The Llano Estacado plain,
In Spain he'd left behind.

Comanche in their majesty,
No finer mounted band.
Swept this endless sea of grass,
As one was horse and man.

Then came the Texas Longhorn,
JA and XIT.
No fence to stop their ranging,
As far as you could see.

Cowboys yes I see them there,
Like mounted knights of old.
Lineage from vaqueros past,
So young and strong and bold.

As tough as leather woven tight,
With hands so strong yet fine.
With riding skills made legend,
What will they leave behind.

Now winds still sweep these open plains,
One thing will never end.
They'll be here forever,
Should we pass this way again.

So as we walk life's pathway,
Our days blend into weeks.
The weeks to years, the years to life,
The hands of time will sweep.

As the end approaches,
Some things we'd do again.
This option isn't offered,
Least not to mortal man.

But timeless is the Llano,
Just passed from man to man.
Upon these plains they leave no mark,
Just ashes in the wind.

Waiting At The Gate

When the final trail is ridden,
When the gates are closed and latched.
When the branding fires are smothered,
And there'll be no looking back.

By then the book of life is closed,
The records have been made.
This life is all behind you,
Do you think you made the grade?

Was you too rowdy in your youth,
Was your heart and soul in line.
Was your life one full of giving,
Did you leave some good behind?

Did you fulfill that promise,
When you was purt near gone.
"Dear Lord just pull me through this
time,
I'll be your faithful son."

That time up there in Waco,
The Brazos brim to brim.
The hand of God sure saved your skin,
He pulled you through again.

When I got throw'd in Fort Worth,
That bronc near stomped my head.
I broke a rib and got beat-up,
Somehow I just ain't dead.

And on the western plains that night,
With cattle wall-to-wall.
His hand was there to catch you,
When your pony took that fall.

So time again he had his chance,
To take your scrawny soul.
I guess the time was never right,
Cause he kept your body whole.

But time wins out as time will do,
You finely wore plumb out.
Your ticker quit you late last night,
You died without a shout.

So here it is the last hurrah,
You're in this ole pine crate.
If there was things you should have
done,
Ole boy, you're just too late.

He's standing there a'waiting,
With tally book in hand.
He guards the gate to heaven,
And He measures every man.

And as them Cowboys stand in line,
He gives them most a nod.
To ride the range that's broad and green,
We're welcomed home by God.

You Know I'll Make A Hand

Some day much sooner than I hope,
From this ole world I'll pass.
I'll meet my maker face to face,
These questions I will ask.

Is it true you bossed the crews,
With the biggest brands of all?
You pushed them Longhorns up the
trail,
And you've heard them doggies bawl?

Was it you that reached to earth,
Grabbed Buck that rainy night?
And saved his neck in that stampede,
He was really in a tight.

When Nick he got himself stomped flat,
He was out for three whole days.
Did you send help or work alone,
His scrawny neck to save?

And when we crossed the raising Red,
That log was floating down.
It hit my horse and knocked me off,
I surely thought I'd drowned.

I recall one winter's night,
The snow was in our face.
Somewhere we saw a guiding light,
Was you there in that place?

Did you turn that frightened herd,
The night the hail stones fell?
If it was, I thank you Sir,
It was like a living hell.

You must have had a busy night,
When the Indians hit the crew.
They could have killed the whole darn
bunch,
If you hadn't pulled us through.

So many times your hand was there,
When our need was oh so great.
Sometimes we didn't help ourselves,
When we played with our own fate.

I know you been a watching me,
For low these many years.
I felt you in my weakness,
You helped me through my fears.

I know your tally book is full,
Don't know why you should care.
But thank you Sir for watching out,
And always being there.

And when we reach the big corral,
And you've approved my brand.
Please make sure I'm on your crew,
Cause you know I'll make a hand.

Educated Cowboys

Cowboys didn't read too good,
Fact most just not at all.
So they was known to memorize,
To help them to recall.

They knowed the brands from far and
near,
The ranch and foreman's name.
They knew the gals from North and
South,
They played some bunkhouse games.

They could stand up straight and tall,
Recite words on a can.
Some could do a Bible verse,
Could do it to a man.

They knew the horse to ride each day,
Fast, or sure at night.
But they was plumb illiterate,
They couldn't read or write.

They knew the clouds, could read the
sign,
To look for storms and rain.
But books was not their strongest suit,
Just stored it in their brain.

Some could cipher, make their mark,
This didn't help 'em much.
Except at round-up tally time,
For counting cows and such.

131

They knew when they had been short-
changed,
When pay day came around.
Two twenty dollar eagles,
Was all that need be found.

They knew the numbers on the cards,
Could read a players hand.
Could see their eyes or watch their tell,
To fold or when to stand.

But most was young and pushing cows,
Instead of reading books.
Riding herd and playing cards,
The school of old hard knocks.

So when we talk of poetry,
Which they would never do.
They'd read it if they only could,
And now you know the truth!

About The Author

Quentin M. Thomas (AKA Texas Red) is a native of Fort Worth, Texas and a retired USAF Colonel. He has had a love for the American West since his youth at the Saturday morning matinees. He has done extensive research on the American West and is an accomplished historian with extensive studies in American history from the civil war era forward. Reared near the Chisholm Trail in Ardmore, Oklahoma he has never been far from the influences of the American cowboy. He has lived across America and savored her heritage, is a published author, business consultant, and frequent speaker on American history.

If you are interested in having Texas Red speak at your meeting or event, e-mail Quentin at thomasgroup@aol.com.